SUMMER SKILLS
for the
1st Grade Graduate

Written by Sally Cardoza Griffith

Annotated Bibliography provided by Sara Freeman

Illustrated by Megan E. Jeffery

Senior Editor: Christine Hood
Editor: Concetta Doti Ryan, M.A.
Inside Design: Rose Sheifer
Cover Design: Joanne Caroselli
Cover Photography: ©1998 Comstock, Inc.

Frank Schaffer Publications
23740 Hawthorne Blvd.
Torrance, CA 90505

Table of Contents

Parent Letter **4**

Making the Most of *Summer Skills* . . . **5**

Fun Everyday Learning Activities . . . **8**

Reading Favorites Children Love . . . **10**

Week 1 . . . . **14**
● Language Arts
(comprehension, initial consonants, verbs, spelling, vocabulary)
● Math
(numerical order, addition)

Week 2 . . . . **21**
● Language Arts
(comprehension, initial consonants, opposites)
● Math
(reading a graph, subtraction, numerical order, telling time)

Week 3 . . . . **29**
● Language Arts
(comprehension, vowel sounds)
● Math
(addition, subtraction, numerical order, money, measurement)

Week 4 . . . . **37**
● Language Arts
(reading, alphabet, punctuation, vowel sounds, letter writing)
● Math
(fractions, counting by 2, addition, telling time)

Week 5 . . . . **45**
● Language Arts
(reading, rhyming words, spelling, vocabulary)
● Math
(counting by 2, patterns, addition, subtraction, money)

Week 6 . . . . **53**
● Language Arts
(comprehension, creative writing, spelling, verb tense)
● Math
(telling time, counting by 5, place value)

Week 7 . . . . **60**
● Language Arts
(comprehension, vowel sounds, spelling)
● Math
(comparisons, measurement, fractions, addition)

Week 8 . . . . **68**
● Language Arts
(reading, picture clues, creative writing, capitalization, punctuation, adjectives)
● Math
(graphing, numerical order, counting by 5, subtraction)

Week 9 . . . . **76**
● Language Arts
(comprehension, vowel sounds, plurals, compound words)
● Math
(addition, counting, place value)

Week 10 . . . . **83**
● Language Arts
(comprehension, vowel sounds)
● Math
(story problems)

Make Your Own Book! **87**

Certificate of Completion **93**

Answer Key **94**

Assessment Overview **97**

Flash Cards and Charts **105**

Dear Parents,

Congratulations! Your choice of this book shows that you are concerned about the education and development of your child. You are willing to go that extra mile to ensure that your child continues to grow and learn over the summer months. Although he or she learns a lot in school, you are your child's most important teacher. Showing your child how important learning is to you will motivate him or her by your example.

Summer vacation is a time for rest, renewal, and good old fun! You want to make sure, however, that your child continues to grow academically during the time he or she is away from the classroom. Ten weeks away from school is a long time, but this time can be used productively to reinforce and maintain the skills your child has worked so hard to learn during the school year. First grade is an incredibly important year in a child's education. Reading, writing, and beginning math skills have been developed, and daily practice in these areas is the key to continued success.

Summer Skills for the 1st Grade Graduate is designed to keep your child's academic skills honed during the summer months. This book isn't designed as a typical textbook. Instead, it offers a series of fun, engaging activities that will delight, challenge, and motivate your child to keep learning as he or she practices essential math, reading, and language arts skills taught in the first grade. When September comes, your child will be ready to leap into second grade!

Show your child that learning is an everyday experience, one that can be fun, adventurous, and challenging. "Take a bow" for demonstrating that you value education and for lending a hand toward the goal of lifetime learning for your child. Best of all, you will be doing it together! Nothing delights your child more than individual attention from his or her favorite adult—you! Your involvement as a partner in your child's education is something to be proud of. So, enjoy the summer, and better yet, enjoy spending this treasured time helping your child learn.

Making the Most of "Summer Skills"

Summer Skills for the 1st Grade Graduate provides an important link between your child's first- and second-grade school year. It reviews what your child learned in the first grade, providing the confidence and skills that he or she needs for the coming fall. The activities in this book will help your child successfully bridge the gap between first and second grade by reviewing and reinforcing the important and essential skills for his or her continued academic success. These activities are designed to

- review skills in math, reading, and language arts that first graders learned the previous year.
- give you an opportunity to monitor your child's skills in various areas.
- offer you a chance to spend special time with your child.
- enable your child to continue routine daily learning activities.
- give you a chance to praise your child's efforts.
- demonstrate to your child that you value lifetime learning.
- make you an active and important part of your child's educational development.

About the Book

This resource contains a myriad of fun and challenging reading, writing, and math activities. The reading and writing pages provide practice in reading comprehension, poetry, grammar, spelling, phonics, and imaginative and practical writing. The math pages review skills taught in first grade, such as basic addition and subtraction facts, counting by twos and fives, patterning, place value, and story problems. In addition, pages 87 through 92 make up a booklet that your child can cut out, staple, and illustrate. The pages at the end of the book include an assessment section plus flash cards and charts that reinforce basic skills. These can be torn out and used for practice again and again.

Most of the activities in the book are designed so that your child can work independently. However, your child will enjoy the activities much more if you work alongside him or her. Make sure to let your child know that this is not a workbook with tests, but a book of fun activities that you can do together. The book is divided into ten weeks, with approximately eight activity pages per week. These activities are divided evenly between math and language arts. Feel free to choose how many per day and in which order you do the activities, but complete the weeks in sequence, since activities become increasingly challenging as the book progresses.

Also included in the book is a Certificate of Completion (page 93). Give this to your child at the end of the summer or when he or she has completed all of the activities in the book. Invite him or her to color the certificate, and then frame it for the whole family to admire. Your child will feel a proud sense of accomplishment.

Getting Started

In order for your child to get the most from the activities in this resource, use these helpful tips to make these learning experiences interesting and, most of all, fun!

- Set aside a time each day for completing the activities. Make it a time when your child will be most ready to learn, and make it a routine.

- Provide a pleasant, quiet place to work. This means no TV or radio in your child's work area. Also make sure there is a sufficient light source.

- Review in advance the activity page(s) your child will complete that session. This way you will be able to familiarize yourself with the lesson as well as what materials will be needed to complete it (e.g., pencil, paper, crayons, scissors). Materials are noted in the upper right-hand corner of each activity page.

- Have your child read directions aloud beforehand to make sure he or she understands the activity. Instructions are written for the child, but he or she may need your help reading and/or understanding them.

- Let your child help choose which activity of the week he or she would like to complete.

- Feel free to reward your child for good effort, but avoid bribing him or her into completing activities.

- Praise all your child's work. It's the effort, not necessarily the end result, that counts most.

Using the Flash Cards

The 40 double-sided flash cards at the back of the book are on perforated card stock. They are easily removed, and are sturdy enough to be used again and again. The first-grade book includes flash cards on opposites, rhyming words, short and long vowel sounds, money, telling time, and addition. Flash cards can be used in a variety of creative and challenging ways:

- Practice sentence making. Have your child choose a word card, then make up a sentence that includes the word.

- Build a "flash-card jail." Have your child sit on the floor and surround him- or herself with the cards. The only way for your child to "escape" is to answer each card correctly!

- Invite your child to race the clock by answering each flash card within a certain time limit. See if he or she can get faster every time!

- Post flash cards all over the house. For example, invite your child to say the answer to a flash card posted on the refrigerator before opening it.

- Hide the cards outside for a "treasure hunt." With each correct answer, give your child a small treat.

- Play a game of "Concentration." Make copies of the cards so you have two of each. Lay the cards face down and draw two. If both of your cards have the same answer, you get to keep the pair!

- Hold a card in your hand and give your partner clues until he or she guesses the problem or word you are holding.

- Play a "travel game." First, place ten cards in a row on the floor or table. The first card is the starting point and the last card is the city or country of final destination. Your child must "travel" along this "route" by reading and answering flash cards correctly. An incorrect answer means your child must place that card back and start over again. The goal is to finish all ten flash cards without stopping. When your child has mastered the first ten cards, move on to the next ten, and so on.

No one knows better than you how your child learns best, so use this book to enhance the way you already work with him or her. Use every opportunity possible as a learning experience, whether making a trip through the grocery store or riding in the car. Pose problems and let your child figure out how to solve them, asking questions such as *Which route should we take to the park? What could we use to make a plant grow straight? How high should we hang this shelf? What color paint best matches our couch?* Also, respond excitedly to discoveries your child makes throughout the day, such as *That rock is really unique! I wonder how long it took the spider to spin that web;* or *You spent your money wisely.* In this way you will encourage and motivate your child to learn throughout the day and for the rest of his or her life, providing the confidence and self-esteem he or she needs for continued academic success.

Fun Everyday Learning Activities

Use these simple educational activities to keep your child's mind engaged and active during the summer months and all year long!

- Read to your child as much as possible. Read books, the comics, or magazines. This is the best thing you can do to develop your child's literacy. When reading, invite your child to read along, looking for clues on the cover and in the pictures. After reading a couple pages, ask your child to predict what will happen next in the story.

- Have your child read to or with you. Using a familiar book, you and your child can each select a character to "be." Then, use special voices to make the characters' words come to life.

- Bake a batch of brownies or cookies together. Have your child read the recipe to you. Then, allow him or her to help measure the ingredients. Cooking provides reading and math practice in one delicious experience!

- Squeeze lemons and make fresh lemonade. While your child stirs, encourage the development of rhythm and rhyme by chanting, *Lemon, lemon, lemonade . . . sweet yet sour, drink it in the shade!*

- Purchase large pieces of colorful sidewalk chalk and draw pictures on the sidewalk or patio. Your child can also practice writing letters and numbers.

- Go to the park and feed the ducks. Have your child dictate a story to you about the ducks, explaining how they came to live at that park, and their relationships to one another. Write down the story in your child's exact words, then invite him or her to draw a picture to go with the text. Save it for the whole family to enjoy!

- Play a quiz show as you drive! In your best game-show-host voice say, *For ten thousand dollars, what's 9 + 3?* or *Which problem do you choose? The problem behind curtain #1, #2, or #3? OOH! You chose curtain #2. That's the hard one. What's 7 + 1 + 2?*, and so on.

- Go to the produce section at the supermarket and make your child aware of the beauty there! Point out the colorful fruit, the strangely-shaped vegetables, and wonder aloud where they all came from. Ask the produce worker to answer questions you or your child may have. Buy a fruit or vegetable you've never eaten before. When you get home, have your child draw it. Then cut it open, smell it, eat it, and describe it!

- Watch an anthill. Observe how the ants carry food and debris in and out of their home. Observe how they touch antennae to communicate. Put a little sugar by the hill and watch what happens. Go to the library and check out a book about ants. Compare what you observed to what you read in the book.

- Collect shells along the beach with your child. Discuss with him or her what each shell could have been, such as *This pink shell was the earring of a princess,* or *This jagged shell was a dragon's tooth.* Have your child use many creative adjectives to develop descriptive skills as well as his or her imagination.

- Invite your child to experiment with colors by painting the bathtub! Buy several different watercolor paints for your child, and let him or her "paint" the bathtub before taking a bath. Invite him or her to mix different colors and describe them. Challenge your child to guess what yellow and red will become, what green and blue will become, and so on. The paint washes right off!

- Practice important information for your child to know, such as your last name, address, telephone number, and emergency numbers.

- Have a camp-out in your backyard! Set up a tent, inviting your child to dictate or write what he or she thinks you will need for the "trip." Stay overnight in the tent and tell stories and sing songs.

- Have a "read and share time" with the whole family. Invite each family member to read silently for a short period of time and then share what was read and how he or she feels about it.

- Take an afternoon summer walk. Ask your child to describe what he or she sees, smells, hears, and feels. Repeat this walk in the evening and ask your child to describe how the sounds, smells, sights, and feelings change with the time of day.

- Fill a jar with fish crackers. Invite your child to guess how many crackers are in the jar. Then, place ten crackers in a baggie and show your child what ten crackers look like, then what 25 crackers look like, and so on. Take the crackers out of the jar and count them to see how close the guesses were. Repeat this activity throughout the summer to hone your child's estimating skills, using jelly beans, buttons, crayons, and so on.

- Bring your child grocery shopping. To work on his or her phonics skills, have your child point out items with names starting with a chosen letter (for example, **p**eas, **p**eanuts, **p**asta, **p**lums).

Reading Favorites Children Love

Picture Books

Abuela by Arthur Dorros (Dutton, 1991). While riding on the bus with her grandmother, or abuela, a girl imagines they are flying over New York City.

Alice Nizzy Nazzy, the Witch of Santa Fe by Tony Johnston (Putnam, 1995). Manuela, a good and brave girl, manages to rescue her sheep from a Baba Yaga-like witch in this fun tale.

Amazing Grace by Mary Hoffman (Dial, 1991). In this outstanding picture book, a young imaginative girl succeeds as the lead in the play *Peter Pan,* though her friends tell her she can't play the part because she is a girl and is black.

Around the Pond: Who's Been Here? by Lindsay Barrett George (Greenwillow, 1996). Two kids look for signs of animals while searching for blueberries in this beautifully illustrated nature book.

Crow Boy by Taro Yashima (Viking, 1955). This thoughtful book tells the story of a child in Japan who is an outcast at school until he is befriended by a teacher.

Eggs Mark the Spot by Mary Jane Auch (Holiday House, 1996). In this entertaining story, Pauline the hen helps catch a thief by using her ability of laying illustrated eggs.

Grandma's Latkes by Malka Drucker (Harcourt Brace Jovanovich, 1992). In this friendly book, a child learns about Hanukkah while cooking latkes with her grandma.

Growing Vegetable Soup by Lois Ehlert (Harcourt Brace Jovanovich, 1987). A father and child grow vegetables and then use them to make soup. Look also for *Planting a Rainbow,* a flower garden book by Ehlert, known for her bold graphic art.

Miss Nelson Is Missing! by Harry Allard and James Marshall (Houghton Mifflin, 1977). Poor-behaved students shape up quickly when their kind teacher is replaced by mean Miss Viola Swamp in this amusing book.

Officer Buckle and Gloria by Peggy Rathmann (Putnam, 1995). Officer Buckle's safety tips get much more interesting when his dog partner Gloria begins acting them out.

The Paperboy by Dav Pilkey (Orchard, 1996). Lovely art complements this detailing of a paperboy and his dog's early-morning rounds.

The Polar Express by Chris Van Allsburg (Houghton Mifflin, 1985). The striking illustrations and enchanting story of a boy's visit to the North Pole make this Caldecott Medal-winning book a classic.

Six-Dinner Sid by Inga Moore (Simon & Schuster, 1991). Sid is cat who needs a lot of food and attention, so he manages to con six different owners into thinking he is theirs alone in this sly, entertaining book.

Stellaluna by Janell Cannon (Harcourt Brace, 1993). Exquisite illustrations bring to life this story of a young bat who is raised by birds.

Tacky the Penguin by Helen Lester (Houghton Mifflin, 1988). Although he can't compete in most ways with his other penguin pals, Tacky still manages to save the day in this laugh-out-loud book.

Easy Readers

The Cat in the Hat by Dr. Seuss (Random House, 1957). It's fun, it rhymes, and it helps children read common words. That's why this book remains a favorite.

Digby by Barbara Shook Hazen (HarperCollins, 1997). A sister explains to her brother what things their dog can and cannot do now that it's older.

Dinosaur Time by Peggy Parish (HarperCollins, 1974). Children will enjoy reading with parents to learn about dinosaurs.

Frog and Toad Are Friends by Arnold Lobel (HarperCollins, 1970). These two good friends make children laugh and think while reading about their escapades.

Henry and Mudge: The First Book by Cynthia Rylant (Bradbury, 1987). This book is part of a friendly series of adventures about a boy and his dog.

In a Dark, Dark Room and Other Scary Stories by Alvin Schwartz (HarperCollins, 1984). This is an illustrated collection of seven fun and not-too-scary stories.

Morris Goes to School by Bernard Wiseman (HarperCollins, 1970). In this volume, Morris the kind-but-not-too-bright moose goes to school so he can learn enough to buy candy.

Mr. Putter and Tabby Pour the Tea by Cynthia Rylant (Harcourt Brace, 1994). This is one of the few easy readers that parents actually enjoy reading over and over with children. In this beginning volume of the series, an elderly man gets an elderly cat for a pet.

Super Cluck by Jane and Robert O'Connor (HarperCollins, 1991). The star of this cheery tale is a chicken from outer space.

There Is a Carrot in My Ear and Other Noodle Tales by Alvin Schwartz (HarperCollins, 1982). These stories about a silly family are guaranteed to make children giggle.

The Turnip retold by Harriet Ziefert (Viking, 1996). This story is a bright, easy-to-read version of the classic folktale.

Chapter Books

Charlotte's Web by E. B. White (HarperCollins, 1952). This wonderful tale of friendship involves Wilbur the pig and his spider friend Charlotte, who saves his life.

The Chocolate Touch by Patrick Skene Catling (Morrow, 1952). In this funny story, everything John Midas eats tastes like chocolate.

Freckle Juice by Judy Blume (Four Winds, 1971). When a boy buys a recipe for freckles from a girl at school, he gets a stomachache rather than freckles.

A Lion to Guard Us by Clyde Robert Bulla (Crowell, 1981). In this fine historical fiction book set in the 1600s, a girl helps her younger brother and sister make their way from London to Virginia to find their father.

Ramona the Pest by Beverly Cleary (Morrow, 1968). Ramona is a spunky kindergartner children love reading about. Follow up with other books in this series to see how Ramona does and doesn't change.

Rip-Roaring Russell by Johanna Hurwitz (Morrow, 1983). This easy-to-listen-to series of books describes the everyday adventures of a boy and his little sister Elisa.

The Stories Julian Tells by Ann Cameron (Pantheon, 1981). This is the first in a series of friendly family books about an adventurous young boy and his brother.

Tingleberries, Tuckertubs and Telephones by Margaret Mahy (Viking, 1995). A shy boy and his detective-inspector granny catch a bad pirate in this amusing book.

Folklore and Mythology

Borreguita and the Coyote retold by Verna Aardema (Knopf, 1991). In this delightful tale from Ayutla, Mexico, a clever lamb figures out a plan to keep a coyote from eating her.

The Gods and Goddesses of Olympus by Aliki (HarperCollins, 1994). This book is a beautifully illustrated introduction to the wonderful stories in Greek mythology.

How Turtle's Back Was Cracked retold by Gayle Ross (Dial, 1995). In this humorous Cherokee tale, Turtle's boasting leads to a narrow escape from the wolves and a cracked back that he still wears today.

The Legend of the Bluebonnet by Tomie dePaola (Putnam, 1983). This Comanche legend tells of how the bluebonnet flower came to cover the Texas hillsides. Read it along with dePaola's *The Legend of the Indian Paintbrush*.

Lon Po Po by Ed Young (Philomel, 1989). Striking panel illustrations highlight this Chinese tale of three sisters who encounter a wolf disguised as their grandmother.

The Mitten adapted by Jan Brett (Putnam, 1989). This is a wonderfully illustrated version of a Ukranian folktale in which a boy's lost mitten becomes the crowded home for an amazing number of animals.

Nine-in-One, Grr! Grr! by Blia Xiong (Children's Book Press, 1989). Illustrations that look like exquisite Hmong story cloths complement this Laotian tale of how a bird tricks a tiger and, therefore, prevents tigers from having too many young.

Once There Were No Pandas by Margaret Greaves (Dutton, 1985). This Chinese legend tells the story of how a girl's sacrifice brings about the black markings of panda bears.

Puss in Boots illustrated by Fred Marcellino (Farrar, 1990). Stunning illustrations accompany this fairy tale by Charles Perrault of a clever and resourceful cat.

A Story, A Story by Gail Haley (Atheneum, 1970). This African tale, which won the Caldecott Medal, tells how Anansi the spider brought stories to the people.

Tops and Bottoms by Janet Stevens (Harcourt Brace, 1995). A busy hare tricks a lazy bear in this gardening tale that has its "roots" in slave stories from the American South.

Poetry

Fathers, Mothers, Sisters, Brothers: A Collection of Family Poems by Mary Ann Hoberman (Little, Brown, 1991). This cheerful set of poems and pictures is fun to share together.

Pass It On: African American Poetry for Children selected by Wade Hudson (Scholastic, 1993). Poems by Langston Hughes, Nikki Giovanni, Eloise Greenfield, and others are warmly illustrated in this outstanding collection.

Side by Side: Poems to Read Together collected by Lee Bennett Hopkins (Simon & Schuster, 1988). This varied collection of poems will create an interest and delight in poetry.

Street Rhymes Around the World edited by Jane Yolen (Boyds Mills, 1992). These 17 bilingual rhymes are each illustrated by an artist from the country of origin.

Where the Sidewalk Ends and *Falling Up* by Shel Silverstein (Harper & Row, 1974). These modern classics include humorous poems and illustrations that invite children to laugh and enjoy poetry.

Informational Books

Bicycle Book by Gail Gibbons (Holiday House, 1995). This fun and informative book tells about bicycles past and present.

Brian Wildsmith's Amazing World of Words by Brian Wildsmith (Millbrook, 1997). A visitor from outer space comes across varied scenes of Earth, each labeled with words.

Count Your Way through the Arab World by Jim Haskins (Carolrhoda, 1987). This is one volume in a series of books that introduces different languages and cultures by teaching numbers from one to ten.

Explore a Tropical Forest by Barbara Gibson (National Geographic, 1989). This beautiful pop-up book describes and illustrates the lush and colorful South American rain-forest plants and animals.

Fiesta U.S.A. by George Ancona (Lodestar, 1995). Color photographs and simple text make this an excellent introduction to a variety of holidays celebrated by Hispanic Americans. These holidays include the Day of the Dead, Las Posadas, and Three Kings' Day.

Flash, Crash, Rumble, and Roll by Franklyn M. Branley (HarperCollins/Crowell, 1985). Bright illustrations complement easy-to-understand text about thunderstorms.

Four-and-Twenty Watchbirds by Munro Leaf (Linnet, 1990). Watchbirds teach children about etiquette while describing all sorts of nasty creatures such as a Plotter, a Borrower, and a Know-It-All.

Henri Matisse by Mike Venezia (Children's Press, 1997). This is one volume in the *Getting to Know the World's Greatest Artists* series, renown for its simple text, lively cartoons, and beautiful color art reproductions.

How Much Is a Million? by David M. Schwartz (Lothrop, Lee & Shepard, 1985). Marvelosissimo the Mathematical Magician uses fun and creativity to explain numbers up to a trillion.

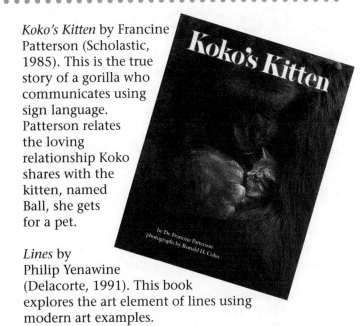

Koko's Kitten by Francine Patterson (Scholastic, 1985). This is the true story of a gorilla who communicates using sign language. Patterson relates the loving relationship Koko shares with the kitten, named Ball, she gets for a pet.

Lines by Philip Yenawine (Delacorte, 1991). This book explores the art element of lines using modern art examples.

Lion Dancer: Ernie Wan's Chinese New Year by Kate Waters and Madeline Lovenz-Low (Scholastic, 1989). Color photographs detail a boy's preparations for being in a Chinese New Year parade.

My Place in Space by Robin and Sally Hirst (Orchard, 1988). In this comic tale, a child know his exact address, including planet, solar system, galaxy, and beyond.

The Popcorn Book by Tomie dePaola (Holiday House, 1978). This book features interesting facts about popcorn.

A Visit to Washington, D.C. by Jill Krementz (Scholastic, 1987). Large color photographs and simple text describing a boy and his family's favorite sites introduce the nation's capital to young children in a wonderful way.

Wilma Unlimited: How Wilma Rudolph Became the World's Fastest Woman by Kathleen Krull (Harcourt Brace, 1996). Bold illustrations augment this inspiring biography of how Wilma Rudolph overcame polio and went on to become an Olympic champion.

At the Park

Read the story. Then answer the questions below.

Jan likes to go to the park. She likes to swing. She likes to climb on the bars. She also likes to slide on the big slide. But, her favorite thing to do at the park is feed the ducks.

Jan often takes bread to the park to feed the ducks. The ducks love to eat the bread! When the bread is gone, Jan pretends she is a duck. "Quack, quack, quack," shouts Jan. "Quack, quack, quack," say the ducks.

1. What are some things that Jan likes to do at the park?

_____

_____

2. What is Jan's favorite thing to do at the park?

_____

3. What does Jan feed the ducks?

_____

4. What does she do when the bread is gone?

_____

5. What is your favorite thing to do at the park?

_____

Phonics Fun!

Write each letter in front of the "ing" ending to create new words. Then read the words and color the pictures.

1. **s**  _____ing

2. **w**  _____ing

3. **r**  _____ing

4. **sw**  _____ing

5. **k**  _____ing

6. **st**  _____ing

Grammar Grabbers

Verbs are words that show action, such as *walk*, *eat*, *fly*, **and** *sleep*. **Add the letters "ing" to each verb in parenthesis. Write the new word on the line.**

1. Jan is _____ on the swings. (swing)

2. The ducks are _____ all the bread. (eat)

3. Now, Jan is _____ like a duck! (quack)

4. All the ducks are _____ to Jan. (walk)

5. One duckling is _____ under his mama's wing. (sleep)

6. The ducks love _____ on the lake. (float)

7. Jan tells the ducks, "I am _____ home, now." (go)

8. As she walks home, she is _____ of all the fun things she will do at the park tomorrow. (think)

 FS23403 Summer Skills for the 1st Grade Graduate © Frank Schaffer Publications, Inc.

Letter Mix-Up

Below are the mixed-up letters of a word. How many little words can you make from this word's letters? Can you make the big word, too?

e s d i l

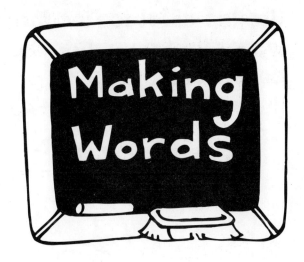

Word with 1 letter:

_____

Word with 2 letters:

_____

Words with 3 letters:

_____

_____

_____

_____

Words with 4 letters:

_____

_____

_____

_____

_____

Word with 5 letters (the BIG word!):

_____

Crossword Fun

Use the clues to find the words that complete the crossword puzzle.

Across

1. metal rails that kids can climb on

3. using your feet and hands to pull yourself up

5. to move smoothly down

8. what ducks say

Down

2. the seat attached to chains that goes back and forth

4. food made out of baked wheat dough

6. body of water with land around it

7. bird that swims and has webbed feet and a bill

Find the Picture

Connect the dots from 1 to 20 to complete the picture. Then color the picture!

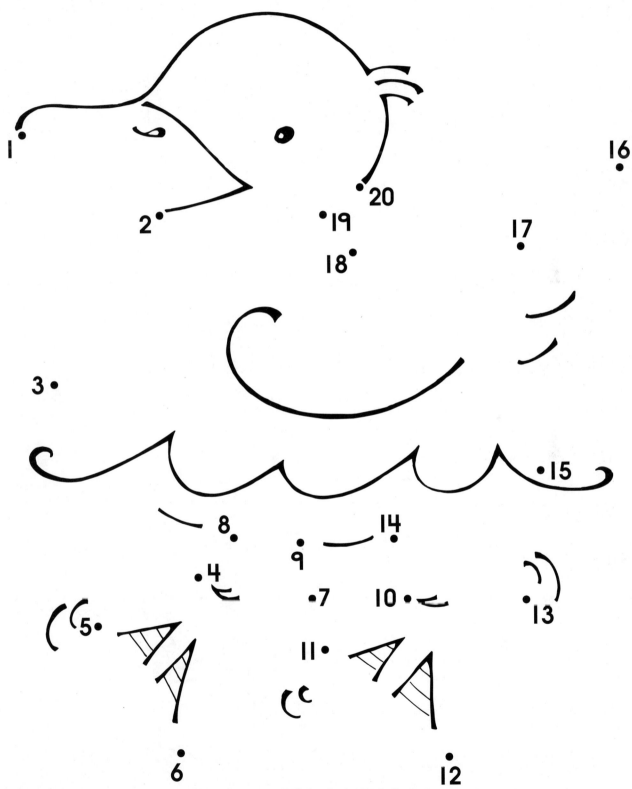

Brain Exercise!

Add to find the answers.

1. 3 + 2 = _____

2. 1 + 3 = _____

3. 0 + 3 = _____

4. 4 + 1 = _____

5. 2 + 2 = _____

6. 1 + 5 = _____

7. 3 + 2 = _____

8. 3 + 4 = _____

9. 4 + 2 = _____

10. 7 + 0 = _____

11. 5 + 2 = _____

12. 0 + 9 = _____

13. 6 + 3 = _____

14. 3 + 5 = _____

15. 2 + 4 = _____

16. 4 + 6 = _____

A Day at the Beach

Read the story. Then answer the questions that follow on pages 21 and 22.

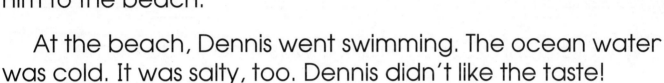

Dennis was happy. It was summer vacation. His mom promised to take him to the beach.

At the beach, Dennis went swimming. The ocean water was cold. It was salty, too. Dennis didn't like the taste!

Dennis played in the sand. He made sand castles. He found lots of pretty shells. He even found some slimy seaweed!

At lunch time, Dennis and his mom ate sandwiches. They drank soda from cans. It was cold. It was sweet. Dennis liked the taste!

After lunch, Dennis took a nap on his towel. The sun made his skin feel hot.

"Time to go home," said Dennis's mom. "Your skin is getting too pink!"

1. Why was Dennis happy?

_____

_____

2. What did Dennis do at the beach?

_____

_____

A Day at the Beach (cont.)

3. Why didn't Dennis like the taste of the ocean water?

_____

4. What did Dennis like to drink? Why?

_____

5. Why did Dennis's mom think it was time to go home?

_____

Draw a picture to show your favorite part of the story. Write a sentence below that tells about your picture.

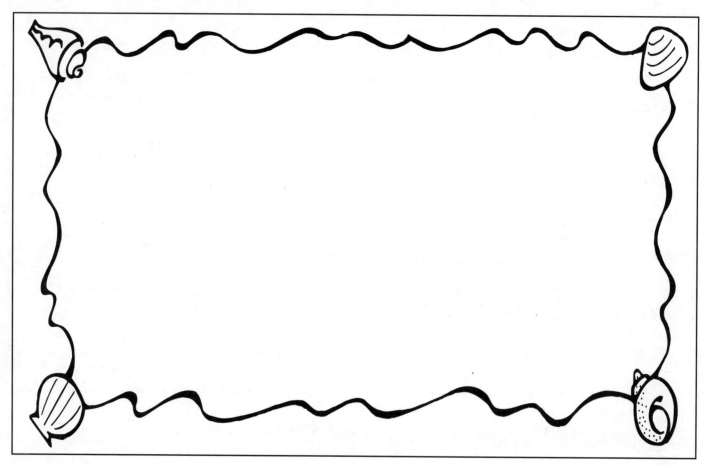

_____

Phonics Fun!

Write the missing letter to complete each word. Then draw a picture to illustrate the word.

1. ___wimming

2. ___eaweed

3. ___un

4. ___and castle

Grammar Grabbers

Read each sentence. Then find the word below that is the opposite of each underlined word. Use the words to finish each second sentence.

wet	smooth	awake	sour	down	hot

1. The soda tasted <u>sweet</u>.

   The lemon tasted _____.

2. Dennis took a nap and fell <u>asleep</u>.

   His mom stayed _____.

3. Summer is warm and <u>dry</u>.

   Winter is cold and _____.

4. The ocean felt <u>cold</u>.

   The bubble bath felt _____.

5. The waves in the ocean go <u>up</u>.

   The waves in the ocean come _____.

6. The sand is very <u>rough</u>.

   A clamshell is very _____.

Favorite Sandwich

Use the graph to answer the questions.

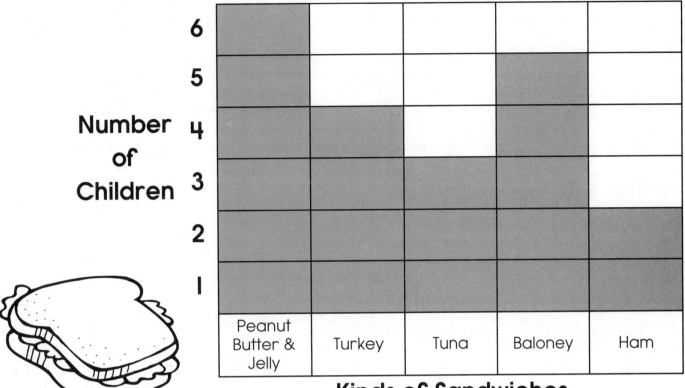

Kinds of Sandwiches

1. Which sandwich is liked by the most children?

   _____

2. Which sandwich is liked by the least children?

   _____

3. How many children like turkey sandwiches? _____

4. How many children like tuna sandwiches? _____

5. Do more children like baloney or turkey sandwiches?

   _____

Brain Exercise!

Subtract to find the answers.

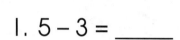
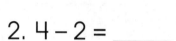

1. $5 - 3 =$ _____

2. $4 - 2 =$ _____

3. $6 - 3 =$ _____

4. $5 - 0 =$ _____

5. $2 - 2 =$ _____

6. $7 - 2 =$ _____

7. $7 - 5 =$ _____

8. $5 - 1 =$ _____

9. $3 - 2 =$ _____

10. $5 - 4 =$ _____

11. $6 - 5 =$ _____

12. $6 - 4 =$ _____

13. $7 - 3 =$ _____

14. $6 - 2 =$ _____

15. $7 - 6 =$ _____

16. $7 - 7 =$ _____

Before and After

Look at the numbers inside each set of shells. What number comes before? What number comes after? Write the missing numbers in the empty shells.

1.

7 ___ 9

2.

11 12 ___

3.

8 9 ___

4.

___ 15 16

5.

___ 1 2

6.

18 ___ 20

7.

13 14 ___

8.

10 ___ 12

What Time Is It?

Dennis has a broken watch. He doesn't want to be late for the beach! Can you fix it for him? Draw the hands on Dennis's watch for each time shown.

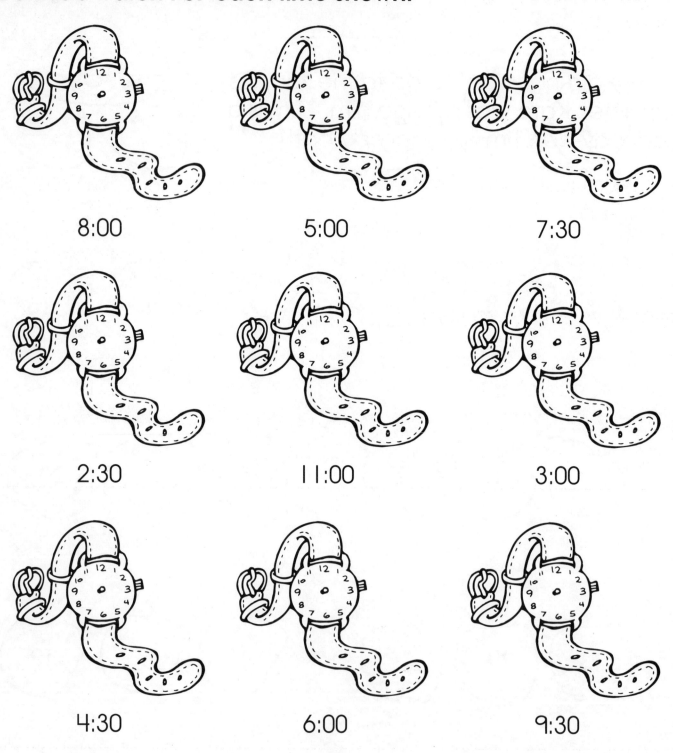

8:00   5:00   7:30

2:30   11:00   3:00

4:30   6:00   9:30

FS23403 Summer Skills for the 1st Grade Graduate   © Frank Schaffer Publications, Inc.

A Snake Story

Read the story, then draw the pictures following the directions. After you read the story, answer the questions on page 31.

Tim did not want to go to the zoo. His big sister Kate was teasing him. "Tim is a scaredy-cat. Tim is a scaredy-cat!"

"I am not!" said Tim. But Tim really was afraid. He was afraid of one kind of animal at the zoo—the snakes.

Tim's dad told him that the snakes were in glass cages and couldn't get out. But that didn't matter to Tim. He didn't even like to look at them.

At the zoo, Tim, Kate, and their dad saw elephants, zebras, alligators, and monkeys. They ate candy and popcorn. Then, Tim saw the scary sign! It said, "SNAKES"!

(Draw the snake sign.)

A Snake Story (cont.)

Kate walked to the cages. Tim's dad held his hand. "You decide, son," his dad said. Tim took a deep breath and said, "Let's go."

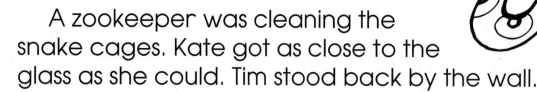

A zookeeper was cleaning the snake cages. Kate got as close to the glass as she could. Tim stood back by the wall.

"Are those snakes slimy?" Kate asked the zookeeper.

"No, they're not," the zookeeper replied. "They feel like your skin. But they have scales, so they feel a bit bumpier."

"What do they eat?" asked Kate as Tim stepped closer.

"They eat live mice," the zookeeper answered.

"Will they hurt me?" asked Tim as he took one last step and placed his face next to the glass cage.

(Draw a picture of Tim looking at the snakes.)

FS23403 Summer Skills for the 1st Grade Graduate

A Snake Story (cont.)

The zookeeper said, "Well, these snakes are safely locked behind the glass. Snakes don't want to hurt anybody. They're just trying to survive. But sometimes people scare them, so they try to defend themselves. That's when people can get hurt."

The zookeeper left, and Tim, Kate, and their dad stared into the cage. The snakes stared back.

"I guess you're not scared anymore, Tim," said Kate.

"Well, once you learn about something, it's not as scary. Besides, they are behind glass!" replied Tim. They all laughed together.

Answer "T" for true or "F" for false.

1. Snakes eat popcorn. _____

2. Snakes are slimy. _____

3. Snakes might hurt you when trying to defend themselves. _____

4. Tim ran away from the snakes. _____

5. After Tim learned about the snakes, he wasn't afraid anymore. _____

Phonics Fun!

Short "a" sounds like the "a" in *candy*.

Long "a" sounds like the "a" in *snake*.

Circle the pictures of the words that have the short "a" sound. Draw an "X" on the pictures of the words that have the long "a" sound.

cake   glass   cat

cage   ant   lake

sandwich   hand   face

Color by Number

Sammy Snake needs some pretty skin. Add or subtract to find the answer for each section. Then match the answer to the color key and color each section.

Color Key
6 = red
7 = orange
8 = yellow

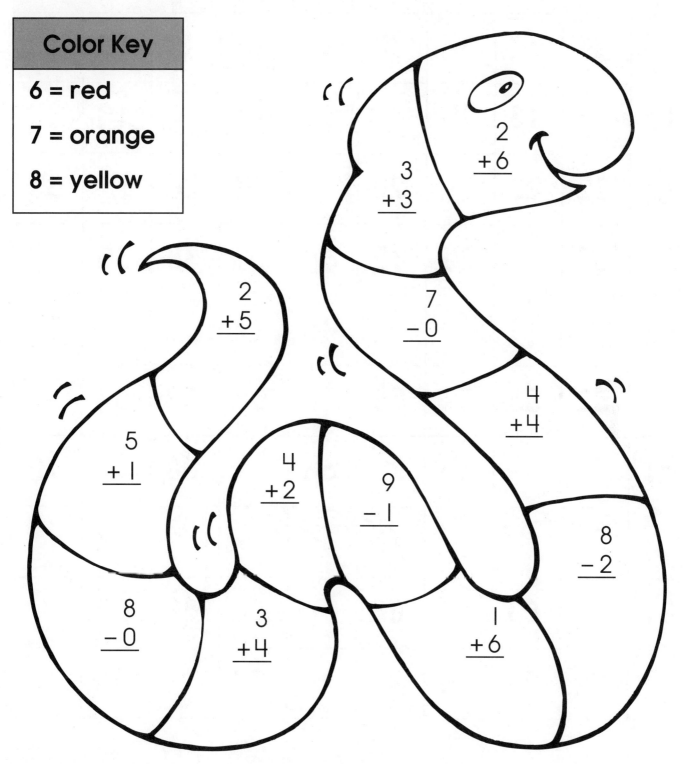

Missing Numbers

Fill in the chart with the missing numbers from 1 to 100. When you're done, read the numbers aloud.

1	2		4	5	6		8	9	10
11		13	14		16	17		19	
	22	23		25		27	28		30
31	32		34	35	36		38	39	
41		43			46	47			50
	52	53	54	55		57	58	59	
61			64		66		68		70
				75				79	
81		83		85			88	89	
	92	93	94			97		99	

FS23403 Summer Skills for the 1st Grade Graduate

Spending Spree!

Tim wants to buy a snack. He has a quarter, which is 25 cents. Which snacks can he buy?

Count the coins needed to buy each snack. Circle "Yes" if Tim has enough money, or "No" if he does not.

1.   Yes   No

2.   Yes   No

3.   Yes   No

4.   Yes   No

Slithering Snakes

Use the unit measurements to measure each snake. Color the longest snake green. Color the shortest snake yellow. Color the middle-sized snake brown.

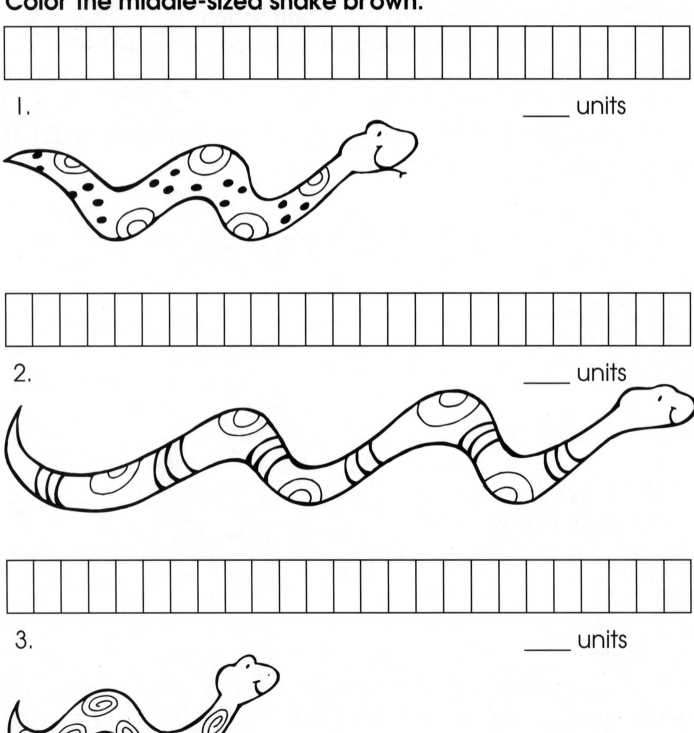

1. ___ units

2. ___ units

3. ___ units

FS23403 Summer Skills for the 1st Grade Graduate

Summer Letter

July 15

Dear Mike,

Hi! I hope your summer is going well. My summer is great! I have been going to the beach a lot. What have you been doing? Have you gone to the pool much?

Did you see that new movie about the dinosaurs? I did. It was cool.

Well, I've got to go. My mom is taking me to the library. We have to get there before it closes. I want to read some books about dinosaurs.

Write back soon!

See ya,

Dennis

P. S. I made this picture for you, but it's not finished yet.

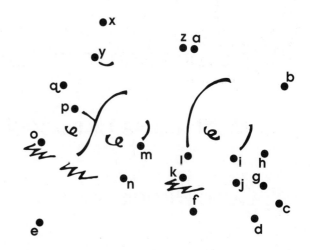

Complete the dot-to-dot from a to z to finish Dennis's picture.

Grammar Grabbers

A statement ends with a period (.). A question ends with a question mark (?). Punctuate each sentence below.

1. Dennis and Mike are good friends ____

2. Has Mike gone swimming in his pool ____

3. What time does the library close ____

4. Dennis wants to read books about dinosaurs ____

5. Can Mike spend the night at Dennis's house ____

6. The dinosaur movie was very good ____

7. It is fun to go to the library ____

8. What movie did Dennis see ____

9. Does Dennis like to draw ____

10. Where does Mike live ____

Phonics Fun!

Short "e" sounds like the "e" in *ten*.

Long "e" sounds like the "e" in *bee*.

Read each word below. If it has the short "e" sound, write it in the "Short e" column. If it has the long "e" sound, write it in the "Long e" column.

beach	hen	eat	bed
feet	red	shell	me
treat	head	spend	sea
when	den	bean	see

Short "e"   **Long "e"**

_____   _____

_____   _____

_____   _____

_____   _____

_____   _____

_____   _____

_____   _____

Write a Letter!

Write a letter to your best friend. Tell him or her about what you've been doing this summer. Ask your friend some questions about what he or she has been doing. Ask your parents to help you mail the letter.

_____
(today's date)

Dear _____,

_____

_____

_____

_____

_____

_____

From,

_____
(your name)

FS23403 Summer Skills for the 1st Grade Graduate

A Piece of the Pie

When you divide something in half, you divide it into two equal parts. Dennis wants to share his snacks equally with Mike. Draw a line on each food to divide it in half. Then color each half differently.

1.

2.

3.

4.

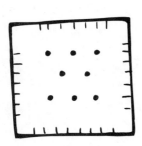

5.

6.

7.

8.

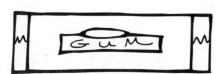

What Comes Next?

Skip-count by 2 to fill in the blanks.

1.   4   ____   8

2.   30   ____   34

3.   12   14   ____   ____   20   22

4.   44   46   48   ____   52   54

5.   22   ____   26   ____   ____   32

6.   54   ____   ____   60   ____   64

7.   80   82   ____   ____   88   90

8.   72   ____   76   ____   ____   82

FS23403 Summer Skills for the 1st Grade Graduate

Brain Exercise!

Add the numbers to find the answers.

1. 2 + 4 + 3 = ___

2. 3 + 1 + 2 = ___

3. 0 + 4 + 4 = ___

4. 5 + 2 + 2 = ___

5. 6 + 1 + 1 = ___

6. 7 + 1 + 1 = ___

7. 3 + 5 + 0 = ___

8. 1 + 4 + 3 = ___

9. 8 + 2 + 0 = ___

10. 4 + 2 + 3 = ___

11. 6 + 3 + 0 = ___

12. 3 + 3 + 1 = ___

13. 5 + 3 + 1 = ___

14. 9 + 0 + 2 = ___

15. 6 + 3 + 3 = ___

16. 4 + 4 + 4 = ___

What Time Is It?

Write the time below each clock.

1. _____ : _____

2. _____ : _____

3. _____ : _____

4. _____ : _____

5. _____ : _____

6. _____ : _____

7. _____ : _____

8. _____ : _____

Imagination

Read the poem aloud. Then answer the questions below.

Summer days are bright and hot,

I eat ice cream and swim a lot.

I'm free to dream that I'm in charge,

of worlds beyond my small backyard.

From outer space to the deepest seas,

I'm the one the world must please,

and from my command post (it's a chair),

I am the ruler of Earth and air!

Answer the questions.

1. What do you like to pretend you are? _____

_____

2. Does the child in this poem sound like someone you
could be friends with? Why or why not? _____

_____

It's Rhyme Time!

Words with the same ending sound are called rhyming words. Words like *cow, now,* and *how* are rhyming words. Read the words in the box. Choose the word from the box that rhymes with each word below, then write it on the line.

cap	thank	sleep	more	made
air	sit	walk	hot	bright

1. night _____

2. store _____

3. stayed _____

4. chair _____

5. drank _____

6. fit _____

7. keep _____

8. lot _____

9. nap _____

10. talk _____

Rhyming Words in Action

Use the words from the box on Page 46 to complete these short poems.

1. Every day the sun is _____.
   It shines on Earth to give us light.

2. The blackbird flies through the _____.
   It's free and happy, without a care.

3. The baby cried, "I want some _____!"
   The daddy cried, "I'm off to the store!"

4. The ocean seems silent, so green and so deep,
   It's almost as if all the animals just _____.

5. You can use the colored chalk
   To write and draw on the side _____.

Letter Mix-Up

Below are the mixed-up letters of a word. How many little words can you make from the letters? Can you make the big word, too?

t   i   r   h   b   g

Word with 1 letter:

_____

Words with 2 letters:

_____

_____

Words with 3 letters:

_____

_____

_____

Words with 5 letters:

_____

_____

Word with 6 letters (the BIG word!):

_____

Blast Off!

Count by 2s to complete the picture and find out where your imagination can take you! Then color the picture.

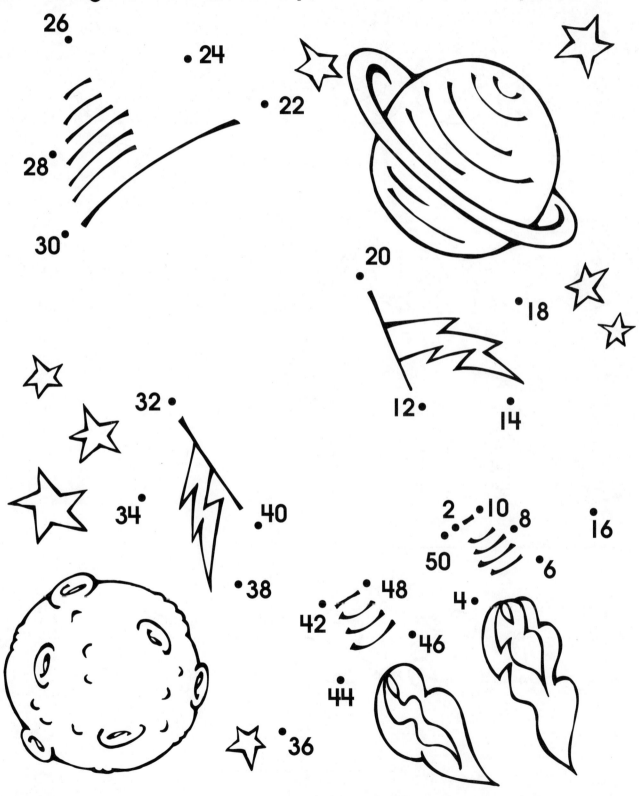

What Comes Next?

Complete each pattern by drawing a picture in the blank.

1.

2.

3.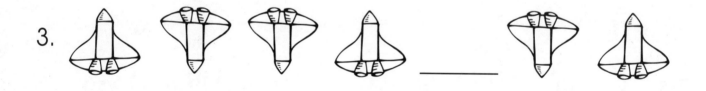

4.

FS23403 Summer Skills for the 1st Grade Graduate

Brain Exercise!

Add or subtract to find the answers.

1. 9 – 2 = ___

2. 10 – 5 = ___

3. 3 + 6 = ___

4. 10 – 7 = ___

5. 5 + 4 = ___

6. 4 + 4 = ___

7. 5 + 5 = ___

8. 3 + 5 = ___

9. 10 – 1 = ___

10. 10 – 8 = ___

11. 6 + 4 = ___

12. 7 + 1 = ___

13. 8 + 2 = ___

14. 1 + 9 = ___

15. 10 – 6 = ___

16. 7 + 3 = ___

17. 0 + 10 = ___

18. 9 – 7 = ___

Spend the Money!

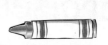

Look at each toy and it's price. Draw a line to match the cost of the toy to the correct amount of money.

On the Farm

Read the story. Then answer the questions that follow.

"Can I really milk the cow?" Robin asked her grandpa. She'd never touched a cow before! Robin was spending two whole weeks with her grandparents on their farm. Her mom and dad had gone away for a vacation and left Robin with her grandparents. She had never been on a farm, and she was the only kid in the house!

"Of course you can milk the cow!" chuckled Grandpa. "Here's how you do it." Grandpa showed Robin how to squeeze the udder. The milk squirted into the bucket below. "Your turn," he said.

Robin held her hands just like Grandpa showed her. She gently tugged, then, *squirt!* The milk went into the bucket! Robin laughed, which startled the cow. The cow MOOED, which startled Robin. Robin jerked her hands, which made the milk squirt all over Grandpa. Grandpa laughed, Robin laughed, and the cow just swished her tail. Robin knew it was going to be a great two weeks!

1. How long was Robin staying with her grandparents?

   _____

2. How did Robin learn to milk the cow?

   _____

Continue Robin's Story

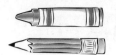

Robin is going to have a lot of fun on her grandparents' farm. What will Robin do after she milks the cow? Will she ride a horse? Will she pick some vegetables? Will she collect eggs from the hens? What will she and her grandparents do next?

Write your own paragraph describing what you think Robin will do next on the farm. When you're finished, draw a picture to match your story.

_____

_____

_____

_____

Written and illustrated by : _____

Letter Mix-Up

Help! The farm animals' names are all mixed up. Help Robin spell them correctly on the line beside each "mixed-up" word.

1. wco : _____

2. sehor : _____

3. eepsh : _____

4. oatg : _____

5. tac : _____

6. terroos : _____

7. nhe : _____

8. ckdu : _____

9. keyrut : _____

10. gdo : _____

11. gpi : _____

Grammar Grabbers

The letters "ed" are added to the end of verbs to show the action happened in the past. Add "ed" to the verb following each sentence. Rewrite the verbs in the blanks to show past tense. (If a word already ends in "e," just add the "d.")

1. Grandma and Robin

   _____ an apple pie.

   (bake)

2. "I _____ milk the

   cows!" said Robin. (help)

3. "What _____ to you?"

   Grandma asked Grandpa.

   (happen)

4. "Robin _____ me instead of the bucket!"

   laughed Grandpa. (squirt)

5. "I already _____ the clothes," said Grandma.

   (wash)

6. "I'll wash it myself. I've already _____ my

   chores for this morning," said Grandpa. (finish)

7. "What's for lunch?" _____ Robin. (ask)

What Time Is It?

Look at the clocks below. Use these examples to help you write the time for each clock.

| 12:00 | 12:15 | 12:45 | 1:00 |

1. ____:____   2. ____:____   3. ____:____   4. ____:____

5. ____:____   6. ____:____   7. ____:____   8. ____:____

FS23403 Summer Skills for the 1st Grade Graduate

Who Moos?

Count by 5s to connect the dots and complete the picture.
Color the picture of the animal in Grandpa's barn!

Grouping by Tens

In the number 10, 1 stands for one group of ten, and 0 stands for the number of extras. For example, in the number 12, there is 1 group of ten and 2 extras.

Look at each number below. Write how many groups of ten and how many extras there are in each number. Use the pictures to help you.

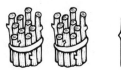

1.　24 = ____ ____
　　　　 tens　extras

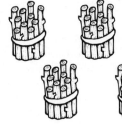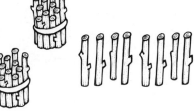

2.　31 = ____ ____
　　　　 tens　extra

3.　58 = ____ ____
　　　　 tens　extras

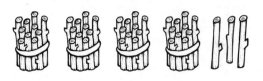

4.　43 = ____ ____
　　　　 tens　extras

5.　16 = ____ ____
　　　　 ten　extras

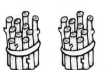

6.　20 = ____ ____
　　　　 tens　extras

A Treasured Book

Read the story. Then answer the questions on the next page.

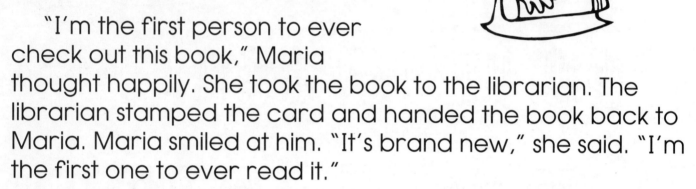

Maria took the book down from the library shelf. It was brand new! The cover was shiny, and the pages were clean.

"I'm the first person to ever check out this book," Maria thought happily. She took the book to the librarian. The librarian stamped the card and handed the book back to Maria. Maria smiled at him. "It's brand new," she said. "I'm the first one to ever read it."

"All books, even the old ones, are treasures, aren't they?" the librarian asked.

Maria thought. "I guess the old ones are even more special," she said.

The librarian looked puzzled. "Why?" he asked.

"Well," answered Maria, "even though this book is pretty and new, you don't know if it is a good story. But, if a book is all worn out, you can tell it's a good one because so many people have read it."

"I guess you're right," the librarian smiled.

"I'll take this book and I'll see if I can find an old one as well," said Maria.

A Treasured Book (cont.)

1. Which book would you rather check out, an old one or a new one? Why?

   _____

   _____

   _____

2. Why did Maria think an old book might be better than a new book?

   _____

   _____

3. Do you agree with Maria that an old book is more special than a new one? Why?

   _____

   _____

4. Which book do you think Maria will like best? Why?

   _____

   _____

Phonics Fun!

Short "o" sounds like the "o" in *hot*.

Long "o" sounds like the "o" in *cold*.

Read each word. If the word has the short "o" sound, write it in red crayon. If the word has the long "o" sound, write it in blue crayon.

go _____   old _____   dot _____

rose _____   got _____   box _____

coat _____   rocket _____   top _____

toad _____   hold _____   hot _____

most _____   boat _____   robin _____

Treasure Hunt

Find the words listed inside the treasure chest in the word search puzzle below.

top	so	clock	goat	pop
note	rock	hot	son	bone

x	z	y	q	r
g	o	a	t	p
h	t	s	o	r
o	p	o	p	o
t	d	n	b	c
c	l	o	c	k
m	b	o	n	e
h	n	o	t	e

More or Less?

Which is more, and which is less? Complete each sentence by writing *more* or *less* on the blank.

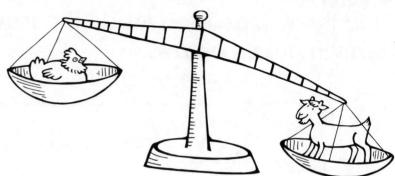

1. 10 – 3 is _____ than 5 + 3.

2. 6 + 4 is _____ than 2 + 7.

3. A man weighs _____ than a boy.

4. A new car costs _____ than a new bike.

5. 5 nickels is _____ than 2 dimes and 7 pennies.

6. 1 quarter is _____ than 3 dimes.

7. A hen weighs _____ than a goat.

8. A gallon of ice cream is _____ than 2 cups of ice cream.

Half for You, Half for Me

When you divide something in half, you divide it into two equal parts. For example, if you have two candy bars and you gave one to your friend, you would have given him or her one-half of what you have.

Color one-half of the items in each group below.

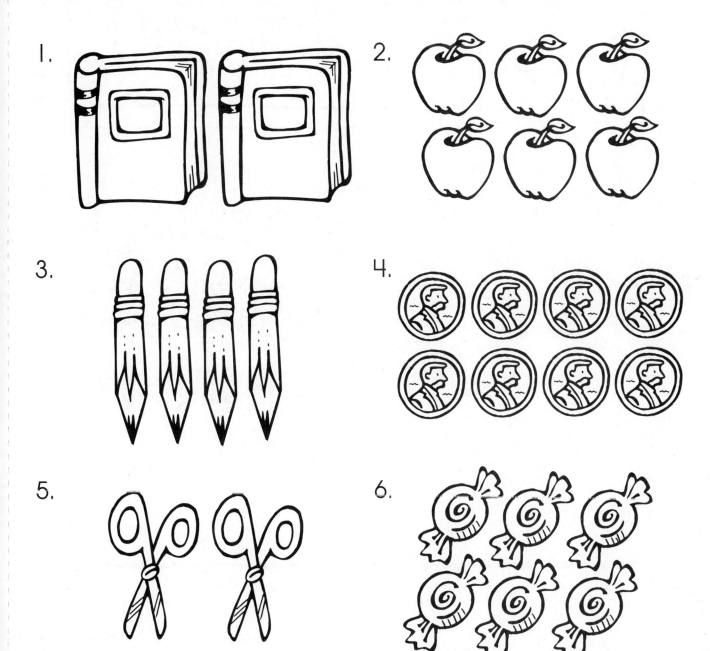

1.

2.

3.

4.

5.

6.

An Inch Is an Inch

Cut the ruler from the bottom of the page. Measure each object to the nearest inch. Write the number of inches on each line.

A. _____

B. _____

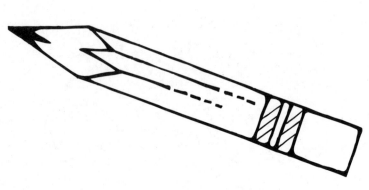

C. _____

D. _____

FS23403 Summer Skills for the 1st Grade Graduate   © Frank Schaffer Publications, Inc.

Brain Exercise!

Add to find the sums.

1. 6 + 4 = _____

2. 6 + 5 = _____

3. 6 + 6 = _____

4. 1 + 10 = _____

5. 8 + 2 = _____

6. 8 + 3 = _____

7. 8 + 4 = _____

8. 2 + 10 = _____

9. 5 + 4 = _____

10. 5 + 5 = _____

11. 5 + 6 = _____

12. 5 + 7 = _____

13. 9 + 1 = _____

14. 9 + 2 = _____

15. 9 + 3 = _____

16. 12 + 0 = _____

17. 11 + 1 = _____

18. 10 + 2 = _____

19. 6 + 3 + 3 = _____

20. 8 + 3 + 0 = _____

For the Birds

Winter, spring, summer, fall,

all the robins do is call,

for spring, summer, fall, winter,

huddled in their nests a-twitter.

Summer, fall, winter, spring,

can't help themselves, they must sing,

through fall, winter, spring, summer,

teaching me to be a hummer.

Hum, hum, hum, hum, hum, hum, hum!

Hum, hum, hum, hum, hum, hum, hum!

Color each picture, then write the season underneath.

_____

_____

_____

_____

FS23403 Summer Skills for the 1st Grade Graduate

Write Away!

This story isn't finished! Use your imagination to finish it. When you've completed your story, give it a title.

_____
(title)

My favorite season is _____ because I

can _____. I can play in the _____

and the _____.

I also like _____ because I can _____

_____.

I don't like _____ because _____

and _____.

Yes, my favorite season is _____.

What's yours?

Grammar Grabbers

Oh, no! These sentences have no capital letters, periods, or question marks. Write each sentence correctly on the line below.

1. can you help fix these sentences

    _____

2. rose checked out many library books

    _____

3. did robin come back from the farm

    _____

4. i think dennis and mike are friends

    _____

5. summer is dennis's favorite season

    _____

Grammar Grabbers

Adjectives are words that describe a person, place, or thing. Circle the adjectives in the sentences below. The first one is done for you.

1. The (frozen) ice cream melted on the (hot) day.

2. Rose liked to read the new book.

3. The cold snow fell on the hard ground.

4. The happy birds sang their cheerful song.

5. The dark forest hid the quiet animals.

6. All the orange and red leaves fell from the big tree.

7. The sunny park was filled with noisy people.

8. Salty water splashed on Dennis's pink face.

9. Robin drank the sweet, creamy milk.

10. The long brown and yellow snake hissed at Tim.

Graph It!

Complete the graph below by asking six people what their favorite season is. Color a square for each response. Start coloring squares at the bottom of the graph first. Then answer the questions below.

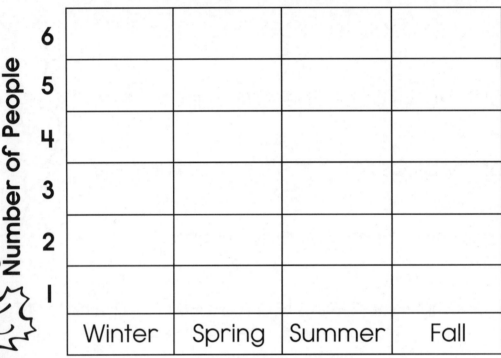

What Is Your Favorite Season?

Number of People	Winter	Spring	Summer	Fall
6				
5				
4				
3				
2				
1				

1. Which season did most of the people like? _____

2. Which season did the fewest people like? _____

3. What did you learn from this graph? _____

_____

4. What can't you learn from this graph? _____

_____

More Numbers Are Missing!

week ⑧

Numerical order, counting by 5

Fill in the chart from 1 to 100. Then count by 5s, and color each fifth square. Explain the pattern.

	2	3		5					10
	12			15			18		20
21			24		26	27		29	
	32	33		35		37	38		40
41			44		46			49	
51	52					57			60
		63	64	65				69	
71	72								
		83			86	87			
91			94		96				100

© Frank Schaffer Publications, Inc.   FS23403 Summer Skills for the 1st Grade Graduate   73

In Reverse

Fill in the missing numbers by counting backwards.

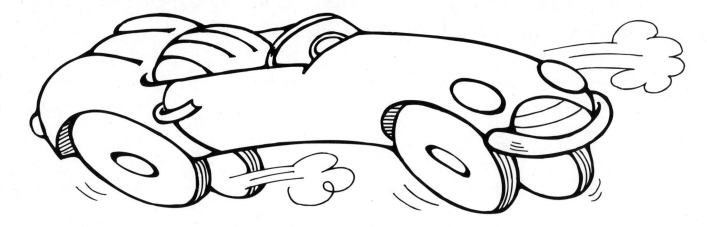

1. 24 ____ 22

2. 12 ____ 10

3. 56 ____ 54

4. 39 38 ____

5. 19 ____ 17

6. 61 60 ____

7. 42 ____ ____ 39

8. 88 87 ____ ____ ____

9. 100 ____ 98 ____

10. 33 ____ 31 ____ ____

11. 30 29 ____ ____ ____

12. 90 ____ 88 ____ ____ 85

13. 45 44 43 ____ ____ ____

14. 82 81 ____ ____ ____

FS23403 Summer Skills for the 1st Grade Graduate

Brain Exercise!

Subtract to find the answers.

1. 10 – 2 = _____

2. 11 – 1 = _____

3. 12 – 1 = _____

4. 8 – 4 = _____

5. 11 – 3 = _____

6. 12 – 2 = _____

7. 11 – 4 = _____

8. 10 – 3 = _____

9. 12 – 3 = _____

10. 11 – 0 = _____

11. 12 – 0 = _____

12. 11 – 5 = _____

13. 12 – 4 = _____

14. 10 – 5 = _____

15. 11 – 6 = _____

16. 12 – 5 = _____

17. 12 – 6 = _____

18. 11 – 7 = _____

19. 11 – 8 = _____

20. 12 – 7 = _____

21. 12 – 8 = _____

22. 10 – 9 = _____

A Ladybug Story

 **Read the story. Then answer the questions that follow.**

Ladybugs are insects. Ladybugs hatch from eggs. As they grow, they change in color from pale orange to red with black spots. Ladybugs eat aphids. Aphids are little green bugs that live on roses and other plants. Ladybugs can fly because they have wings. The red part of a ladybug's body is called the "wing case." They do not fly very fast. Ladybugs sleep through the winter under piles of leaves. In the spring, ladybugs wake up. Time to get busy, ladybugs!

1. What are ladybugs? _____

2. What do ladybugs eat? _____

3. What are aphids? _____

4. What is the red part of a ladybug's body called?

_____

5. What do ladybugs do during the winter? _____

_____

Phonics Fun!

Short "u" sounds like the "u" in *bug*.

Long "u" sounds like the "u" in *unicorn*.

Read each word in the box below. If the word has the short "u" sound, write it in a spot on the ladybug's left wing. If the word has the long "u" sound, write it in a spot on the ladybug's right wing.

summer
June
use
duck
fun
lunch
true
blue
chuckle
cute

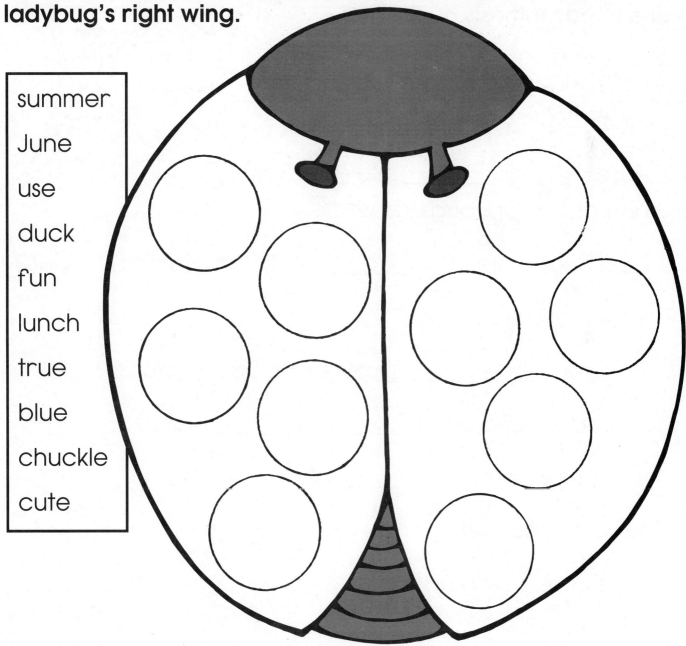

Grammar Grabbers

Singular means one, and *plural* means more than one. To make a word plural, add the letter "s" to the end *(duck = ducks)*. However, if a word ends in *ch, sh, s,* or *x,* add "es" to make the word plural *(fox = foxes)*. Write the plural form of each noun in parenthesis on the line.

1. Ladybugs eat _____.
   (aphid)

2. Rose _____ are good homes for ladybugs. (bush)

3. Ladybugs have _____ to help them fly. (wing)

4. How many bugs are in the _____? (box)

5. The girl _____ bugs in a dish. (catch)

6. The bugs climb on the _____. (dish)

7. Ladybugs have black _____. (spot)

   Extra Challenge!

8. Ladybugs sleep under _____. (leaf)

FS23403 Summer Skills for the 1st Grade Graduate

Grammar Grabbers

A compound word is one big word made up of two smaller words. The word *ladybug* is a compound word. Draw a line to match the words on the left with the words on the right to make compound words.

1. butter   fighter

2. note   bread

3. lady   house

4. corn   fly

5. cup   book

6. fire   bug

7. school   cake

Count the Dots

Add the dots on each ladybug's left wing to the dots on its right wing. Write the addition problem on the first line and the sum on the second line.

1. _____
_____

2. _____
_____

3. _____
_____

4. _____
_____

5. _____
_____

6. _____
_____

7. _____
_____

8. _____
_____

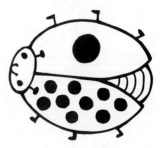

       FS23403 Summer Skills for the 1st Grade Graduate

Catch the Bugs!

Circle each group of ten bugs. Count the extras. Write the numbers on the lines. The first one is done for you.

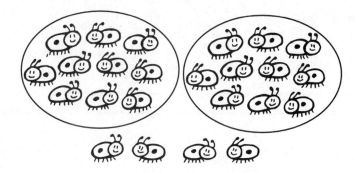

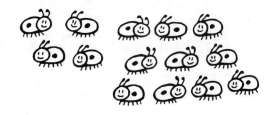

1. __2__ __4__ = _24 bugs_
     tens extras

2. ____ ____ = _____
     ten   extras

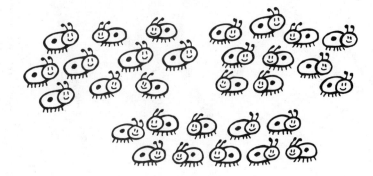

3. ____ ____ = _____
     tens extras

4. ____ ____ = _____
     ten   extra

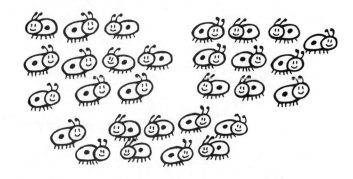

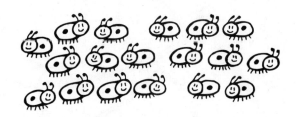

5. ____ ____ = _____
     tens extras

6. ____ ____ = _____
     ten   extras

Who's Hiding?

Find the answer for each problem. Then color each section according to the color key to find who's hiding!

Color Key			
9 = green	10 = blue	11 = black	12 = red

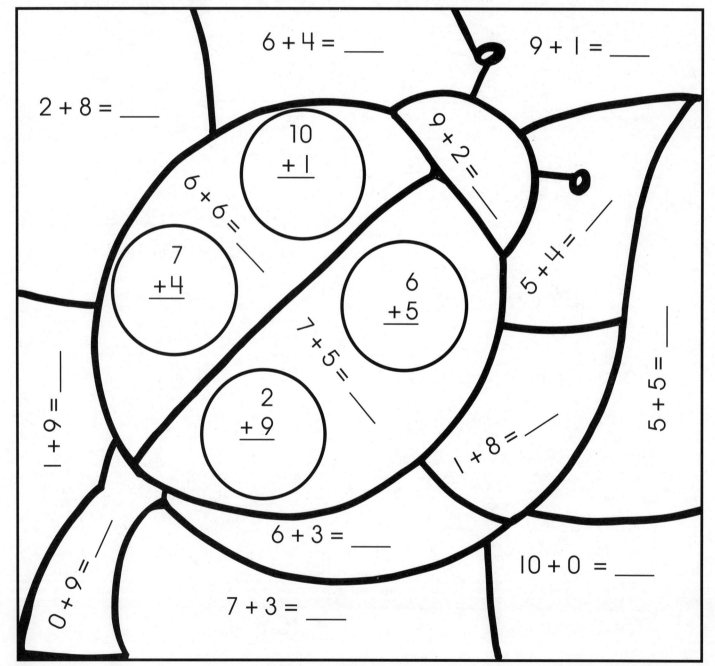

6 + 4 = ___

9 + 1 = ___

2 + 8 = ___

$$\begin{array}{r} 10 \\ +1 \\ \hline \end{array}$$

9 + 2 = ___

6 + 6 = ___

$$\begin{array}{r} 7 \\ +4 \\ \hline \end{array}$$

5 + 4 = ___

$$\begin{array}{r} 6 \\ +5 \\ \hline \end{array}$$

7 + 5 = ___

$$\begin{array}{r} 2 \\ +9 \\ \hline \end{array}$$

5 + 5 = ___

1 + 9 = ___

1 + 8 = ___

6 + 3 = ___

0 + 9 = ___

10 + 0 = ___

7 + 3 = ___

FS23403 Summer Skills for the 1st Grade Graduate

Lilly's New Bike

Read the story. Then answer the questions that follow on pages 83 and 84.

   Lilly was excited. School was going to start in one week, and she would see her friends Jan, Tim, Dennis, Rose, and Robin. She couldn't wait to tell them what she did during the summer! She helped take care of her baby brother and did extra housework for her parents. She also helped her neighbor, Mrs. Hill, wash her car every Saturday. Lilly earned enough money to buy a new bike!

   Lilly's new bike was silver with a red stripe. She was going to ride it to school every day. Now she wouldn't have to walk to school anymore!

   "I guess it really pays to do a job well," Lilly thought. Then she fastened her helmet, hopped on her bike, smiled a big grin . . . and away she rode!

1. Who are Lilly's friends? _____

2. What kind of person do you think Lilly is? Why? _____

_____

Lilly's New Bike (cont.)

3. What kinds of jobs did Lilly do to earn money?

_____

4. Are there certain jobs you do well? Which job is your favorite? Which job do you like the least?

_____

Imagine that you want to earn money by doing special jobs at home or for a friend. Think about which jobs you do well and why someone should "hire" you. Fill in and color the advertisement below to convince someone to give you the job(s) you want.

Hi! My name is _____.

I am ____ years old. I am a good worker.

I'm really good at _____

because _____.

I am willing to do this job for you. I charge

$_____ an hour. You won't find a better

offer anywhere!

FS23403 Summer Skills for the 1st Grade Graduate

Phonics Fun!

Short "i" sounds like the "i" in *insect*.

Long "i" sounds like the "i" in *kite*.

Read each word in the box. If the word has the short "i" sound, write it inside Mrs. Hill's car. If the word has the long "i" sound, write it outside the car. Then color the picture.

smile	hill	excited	stripe	hire
Lilly	bike	silver	thin	ride

Think It Through

Read each story problem. Use your addition or subtraction facts to find each answer. Write the answer as a sentence. The first problem is done for you.

1. Lilly washed Mr. Hill's car on Saturday. He paid her 2 dollars. She washed her mom's car on Sunday. Lilly's mom paid her 2 dollars. How much money did Lilly earn?

   2 + 2 = 4

   Lilly earned 4 dollars.

2. Lilly rode her bike for 3 hours on Monday and 5 hours on Tuesday. How long did she ride her bike all together?

   _____

3. Lilly washed the dishes for her dad. She washed 4 plates, 2 glasses, and 5 bowls. How many dishes did she wash all together?

   _____

4. Lilly was putting 12 cups away. She dropped 6. Crash! How many cups were left?

   _____

Make Your Own Book!

Help your child create his or her own book! Simply cut apart the pages on the dotted lines, place them in numerical order, and staple them together. Read the text to your child, and then ask him or her to read it with you. Invite your child to draw a picture to go with the text on each page. Then he or she will have his or her very own self-made book that can be read over and over!

Ready for Second Grade!

Illustrated by: _____

(your name)

The bell rang. It was time to start second grade. Mike and Lilly were nervous. Would they remember anything from first grade? "I've been practicing my reading and writing all summer," Mike said.

FS23403 Summer Skills for the 1st Grade Graduate

They went into class and sat down. They waved to their friends. Tim poked Mike in the back with his pencil. "Are you ready for second grade?" he asked. "I hope so," said Mike.

2

"I'm writing about the beach," said Dennis. "I'm going to write about the day I got my new bike!" Lilly replied happily.

The teacher, Mr. Clark, said, "Good morning. Welcome to second grade. I'd like you to write about the best day you had this summer. Then draw a picture to go with it."

3

"I'm writing about the day I went to the zoo," said Tim. "I'll write about the park," said Jan.

FS23403 Summer Skills for the 1st Grade Graduate

"I'll write about the days I spent at the library," smiled Rose. They all got busy writing and drawing. Mike sat very still. He was trying to think of something to write about.

6

"That's easy. I'll write about the day I milked cows," Robin said. "What are you writing about, Mike?" Mike looked up and grinned.

Just then, Robin came in and sat next to him. "I'm sorry I'm late, Mr. Clark. I just got back from the farm," she said. Mr. Clark told her to write about her favorite summer day.

7

"I'm writing about the day I got my first letter from Dennis," he replied. "We wrote every week. I'm glad because it helped me practice my reading and writing all summer. Now I know I'm ready for second grade!"

9

Congratulations!

_____

has finished all the
Summer Skills activities!

Now you are ready
for second grade!

FS23403 Summer Skills for the 1st Grade Graduate

Answer Key

Page 14
1. Jan likes to swing, climb on the bars, slide on the big slide, and feed the ducks.
2. Feed the ducks.
3. Jan feeds the ducks bread.
4. Jan pretends she is a duck.
5. Answers will vary.

Page 15
1. sing
2. wing
3. ring
4. swing
5. king
6. sting

Page 16
1. swinging
2. eating
3. quacking
4. walking
5. sleeping
6. floating
7. going
8. thinking

Page 17
1 letter: I
2 letters: is
3 letters: lie, die, lid, led
4 letters: lies, dies, deli, sled, slid, lids, side
5 letters: slide

Page 18

		¹b	a	r	²s				
					w				
		³c	l	i	m	⁴b			
			n			r			
			g			e			
						a			
		⁵s	⁶l	i	d	e			
		⁷d		a					
	⁸q	u	a	c	k				
		c		e					
		k							

Page 20
1. 5
2. 4
3. 3
4. 5
5. 4
6. 6
7. 5
8. 7
9. 6
10. 7
11. 7
12. 9
13. 9
14. 8
15. 6
16. 10

Pages 21 and 22
1. Because it was summer vacation and his mom promised to take him to the beach.
2. Dennis went swimming, played in the sand, made sand castles, found shells and seaweed, ate lunch, and took a nap.
3. Because it was salty.
4. Because it was cold and sweet.
5. Because Dennis's skin was getting too pink.

Page 23
1. swimming
2. seaweed
3. sun
4. sand castle

Page 24
1. sour
2. awake
3. wet
4. hot
5. down
6. smooth

Page 25
1. peanut butter and jelly
2. ham
3. four
4. three
5. baloney

Page 26
1. 2
2. 2
3. 3
4. 5
5. 0
6. 5
7. 2
8. 4
9. 1
10. 1
11. 1
12. 2
13. 4
14. 4
15. 1
16. 0

Page 27
1. 8
2. 13
3. 10
4. 14
5. 0
6. 19
7. 15
8. 11

Page 28

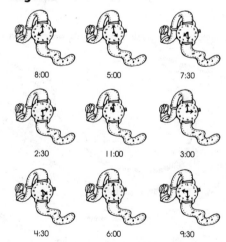

8:00 5:00 7:30
2:30 11:00 3:00
4:30 6:00 9:30

Page 31
1. F
2. F
3. T
4. F
5. T

Page 32
Short a: glass, cat, ant, sandwich, hand
Long a: cake, cage, lake, face

Page 33

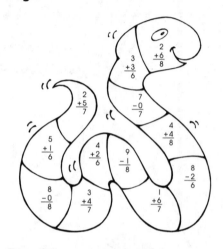

Page 34

1	2	3	4	5	6	7	8	9	10
11	12	13	14	15	16	17	18	19	20
21	22	23	24	25	26	27	28	29	30
31	32	33	34	35	36	37	38	39	40
41	42	43	44	45	46	47	48	49	50
51	52	53	54	55	56	57	58	59	60
61	62	63	64	65	66	67	68	69	70
71	72	73	74	75	76	77	78	79	80
81	82	83	84	85	86	87	88	89	90
91	92	93	94	95	96	97	98	99	100

Page 35
1. yes
2. no
3. yes
4. yes

Page 36
1. 15 units (brown)
2. 25 units (green)
3. 10 units (yellow)

Page 38
1. Dennis and Mike are good friends.
2. Has Mike gone swimming in his pool?

Answer Key

3. What time does the library close?
4. Dennis wants to read books about dinosaurs.
5. Can Mike spend the night at Dennis's house?
6. The dinosaur movie was very good.
7. It is fun to go to the library.
8. What movie did Dennis see?
9. Does Dennis like to draw?
10. Where does Mike live?

Page 39
Short e: hen, bed, red, shell, head, spend, when, den

Long e: beach, eat, feet, me, treat, sea, bean, see

Page 41

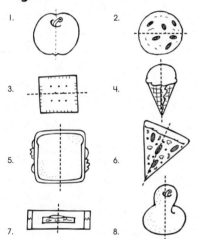

Page 42
1. 6
2. 32
3. 16, 18
4. 50
5. 24, 28, 30
6. 56, 58, 62
7. 84, 86
8. 74, 78, 80

Page 43
1. 9
2. 6
3. 8
4. 9
5. 8
6. 9
7. 8
8. 8
9. 10
10. 9
11. 9
12. 7
13. 9
14. 11
15. 12
16. 12

Page 44
1. 11:30
2. 1:00
3. 2:30
4. 6:30
5. 4:00
6. 12:00
7. 5:30
8. 3:30

Page 46
1. bright
2. more
3. made
4. air
5. thank
6. sit
7. sleep
8. hot
9. cap
10. walk

Page 47
1. bright
2. air
3. more
4. sleep
5. walk

Page 48
1 letter: I
2 letters: it, hi
3 letters: hit, bit, big, rig, rib
5 letters: girth, birth, right
6 letters: bright

Page 50
1. rocket ship
2. star
3. rocket ship pointing down
4. helmet

Page 51
1. 7
2. 5
3. 9
4. 3
5. 9
6. 8
7. 10
8. 8
9. 9
10. 2
11. 10
12. 8
13. 10
14. 10
15. 4
16. 10
17. 10
18. 2

Page 52

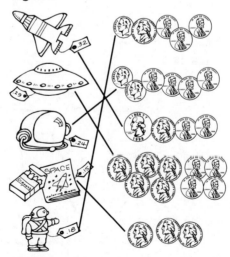

Page 53
1. Two weeks
2. Her grandpa showed her how to squeeze the udder.

Page 55
1. cow
2. horse
3. sheep
4. goat
5. cat
6. rooster
7. hen
8. duck
9. turkey
10. dog
11. pig

Page 56
1. baked
2. helped
3. happened
4. squirted
5. washed
6. finished
7. asked

Page 57
1. 7:00
2. 7:15
3. 7:45
4. 8:00
5. 3:30
6. 3:45
7. 3:15
8. 3:00

Page 59
1. 24 = 2 tens, 4 extras
2. 31 = 3 tens, 1 extra
3. 58 = 5 tens, 8 extras
4. 43 = 4 tens, 3 extras
5. 16 = 1 ten, 6 extras
6. 20 = 2 tens, 0 extras

Page 62
Short o (red): dot, got, box, rocket, top, hot, robin

Long o (blue): go, old, rose, coat, toad, hold, most, boat

Page 63

x	z	y	q	r
g	o	a	t	p
h	t	s	o	r
o	p	o	p	o
t	d	n	b	c
c	l	o	c	k
m	b	o	n	e
h	n	o	t	e

Page 64
1. less
2. more
3. more
4. more
5. less
6. less
7. less
8. more

Page 65
A. 2 inches
B. 4 inches
C. 4 inches
D. 3 inches

Answer Key

Page 66
1. one book
2. 3 apples
3. 2 pencils
4. 4 pennies
5. 1 scissors
6. 3 candies

Page 67
1. 10
2. 11
3. 12
4. 11
5. 10
6. 11
7. 12
8. 12
9. 9
10. 10
11. 11
12. 12
13. 10
14. 11
15. 12
16. 12
17. 12
18. 12
19. 12
20. 11

Page 70
1. Can you help fix these sentences?
2. Rose checked out many library books.
3. Did Robin come back from the farm?
4. I think Dennis and Mike are friends.
5. Summer is Dennis's favorite season.

Page 71
2. new
3. cold, hard
4. happy, cheerful
5. dark, quiet
6. orange, red, big
7. sunny, noisy
8. salty, pink
9. sweet, creamy
10. long, brown, yellow

Page 73
(See answers for page 34.)

Page 74
1. 23
2. 11
3. 55
4. 37
5. 18
6. 59
7. 41, 40
8. 86, 85, 84
9. 99, 97
10. 32, 30, 29
11. 28, 27, 26
12. 89, 87, 86
13. 42, 41, 40
14. 80, 79, 78

Page 75
1. 8
2. 10
3. 11
4. 4
5. 8
6. 10
7. 7
8. 7
9. 9
10. 11
11. 12
12. 6
13. 8
14. 5
15. 5
16. 7

17. 6
18. 4
19. 3
20. 5
21. 4
22. 1

Page 76
1. Ladybugs are insects.
2. They eat aphids.
3. Aphids are little green bugs.
4. It is called a wing case.
5. They sleep under piles of leaves.

Page 77
Short u: summer, fun, chuckle, duck, lunch

Long u: use, true, June, blue, cute

Page 78
1. aphids
2. bushes
3. wings
4. boxes
5. catches
6. dishes
7. spots
8. leaves

Page 79
1. butterfly
2. notebook
3. ladybug
4. cornbread
5. cupcake
6. firefighter
7. schoolhouse

Page 80
1. $3 + 7 = 10$
2. $6 + 5 = 11$
3. $8 + 4 = 12$
4. $5 + 4 = 9$
5. $0 + 11 = 11$
6. $3 + 6 = 9$
7. $4 + 4 = 8$
8. $9 + 1 = 10$

Page 81
2. 1 ten, 4 extras = 14 bugs
3. 3 tens, 0 extras = 30 bugs
4. 1 ten, 1 extra = 11 bugs
5. 2 tens, 9 extras = 29 bugs
6. 1 ten, 8 extras = 18 bugs

Page 82

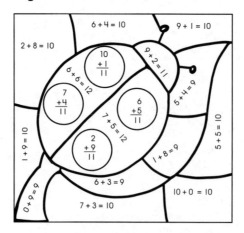

Pages 83 and 84
1. Lilly's friends are Jan, Tim, Dennis, Rose, and Robin.
2. Answers will vary.
3. Lilly took care of her brother, she did extra housework, and she helped her neighbor wash her car.
4. Answers will vary.

Page 85
Short i: hill, Lilly, silver, thin

Long i: smile, excited, stripe, hire, bike ride

Page 86
2. $3 + 5 = 8$;
Lilly rode her bike for 8 hours.
3. $4 + 2 + 5 = 11$;
Lilly washed 11 dishes.
4. $12 - 6 = 6$;
Six cups were left.

FS23403 Summer Skills for the 1st Grade Graduate © Frank Schaffer Publications, Inc.

Assessment Overview

Thinking about Assessment

Parents assess their children all the time by carefully observing them and asking questions. When a baby is asked "Can you say bye-bye?" he or she is being assessed. Asking a child to "Please bring me the green plate" can be seen as an assessment of motor skills, listening skills, and color identification. Your child's progress can be assessed in many different ways.

This booklet contains tools to help you assess some of the important skills that children learn in first grade. They can help you see what your child has learned during the school year and retained during vacation periods. The "Beginning of Summer Pretest" and the "End of Summer Posttest" are two of those tools. The additional activities on this page will also help you review skills in an informal, kid-friendly way.

Here are a few tips to make a test situation as positive and comfortable for a child as possible.

- Read over the test ahead of time, so that you are familiar with what it asks.
- Provide a quiet place to work with few distractions.
- Keep it fun and make sure that your child feels successful. Use praise.
- If your child is stuck on a question, move on to something else. Take note of what the question was.
- Also note how your child approaches questions. This can give you an idea of how your child solves problems.
- Finish on a positive note. Go back to a question your child got right and ask about it, using praise.

How to Use the Tests

The "Beginning of Summer Pretest" is designed to be used at the completion of first grade and before your child completes the activities in the Summer Skills book. It will give you a starting point. Use the "End of Summer Posttest" after the book is completed to assess the skills that have been reviewed.

Parents know that the extra attention they give their children is beneficial in many ways. The time children spend on school-related tasks like those in this book and test booklet can be valuable to both parents and children.

Sight Words

The following is a list of sight words commonly used in first grade reading material. The emphasis is on learning these words so they can be read instantly "by sight."

about	fall	letter	read
after	far	like	red
all	five	little	right
and	found	look	said
any	for	love	sat
away	from	make	school
ball	funny	man	see
be	get	more	so
because	good	mother	such
before	had	myself	take
big	happy	name	three
book	has	next	up
box	have	night	us
came	help	now	very
color	hot	off	was
could	house	on	we
car	if	one	were
carry	it	people	what
did	in	play	when
down	into	please	who
don't	jump	pretty	yes
each	kind	put	yellow
end	know	ran	

Beginning-of-Summer Pretest

Fill in the circle next to the best word.

1. The opposite of <u>slow</u> is
   - ○ slide
   - ○ slower
   - ○ fast

2. The opposite of <u>catch</u> is
   - ○ run
   - ○ throw
   - ○ baseball

3. A word that rhymes with <u>hair</u>
   - ○ car
   - ○ where
   - ○ rain

4. A word that rhymes with <u>tile</u>
   - ○ smile
   - ○ tall
   - ○ male

Circle the two words that make a compound word. Write the word.

5. red   bow   rain   bug

   _____

6. store   star   fire   fish

   _____

Fill in the circle under the word that shows action.

7. Joe is looking for his lunch.
       ○   ○   ○

Fill in the circle under the word that describes a person, place, or thing.

8. My little puppy likes you.
         ○   ○   ○

Beginning-of-Summer Pretest

Read the story. Circle true or false to answer the questions.

Winter is coming. Some animals sleep all winter. This rabbit does not sleep. She makes trails through the brush. Under the snow she finds plants and grass to eat.

9. Rabbits make trails through the brush.

     true   false

10. This rabbit can't find food in the winter.

     true   false

11. Some animals sleep through the winter.

     true   false

Read the story. Find the best picture to go with the story. Trace the picture box.

Ben likes to swim. This summer he learned to go underwater. He can throw a toy in the pool and go get it.

12.

Circle the words that have long vowel sounds.

13. bone    fox   kite   pin

tube    bug   cake    cap

Beginning-of-Summer Pretest

Use abc order to write the missing letters.

14. b ___ d   15. J ___ L   16. n ___ p   17. S ___ U

Fill in the circle next to the word that is spelled correctly.

18. ○ gote
    ○ goat

19. ○ sled
    ○ sleb

Read each sentence. Write the missing punctuation mark.

20. I went to the book fair__   21. Did you go, too__

Write the missing numbers.

22. 11 __ 13   23. 29 __ 31   24. 58 __ 60   25. 35 __ 37

Add or subtract to find the answers.

26. $4 + 0 =$ __   27. $7 + 5 =$ __

28. $4 + 4 =$ __   29. $3 + 2 + 7 =$ __

30. $6 - 4 =$ __   31. $11 - 3 =$ __

Write the time.

32. ___:___   33. ___:___   34. ___:___

Count the money. Circle the correct amount.

35.   22¢   40¢   17¢

End-of-Summer Posttest

Read the story. Answer the questions.

Mother Raccoon is waiting for night. She knows where the corn grows. Tonight she will show her kits how to climb up the stalks and pull down the corn. The raccoons will eat, eat, eat!

1. Fill in the circle by the best title.

   ○ How to Eat Corn   ○ Big Night   ○ Raccoons' Feast

2. What is a kit?

   ○ a corn stalk   ○ a young raccoon   ○ a mother raccoon

3. When do raccoons come out to eat?

   ○ at night   ○ in the day   ○ when the cows leave

Write the missing letters in each word.

4. _ _ ide 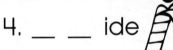   5. l i _ _ t   6. r _ _ n

Read the words in each box. Circle both words if they rhyme.

7.
sleep	miss	pan	pole	air	chalk
keep	mice	pane	mole	care	talk

Write the short vowel.

8. gl _ ss   9. h _ n    10. b _ g

Write the long vowel.

11. c _ ge   12. f _ _ t   13. c _ be

End-of-Summer Posttest

Fill in the circle next to the best word.

14. The opposite of <u>dry</u> is
    ○ cold   ○ desert   ○ wet

15. The opposite of <u>smooth</u> is
    ○ short   ○ rough   ○ hot

Draw lines to make compound words.

16. cup   book
    note   cake
    cow   boy

Fill in the circle under the word that shows action.

17. A cat is sleeping on the rug.

Fill in the circle under the word that describes.

18. His bird sings a happy song.

Fill in the circle by the word that is spelled correctly.

19. ○ clime   20. ○ lake
    ○ climb   ○ lack

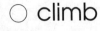 

Use abc order to write the missing letters.

21. d e f __ h __ j k l __   22. P __ R S __ __ V __

FS23403 Summer Skills for the 1st Grade Graduate

End-of-Summer Posttest

Write the missing punctuation marks.

23. This is my book__

24. Which book do you have__

Write the missing numbers.

25. 14   15   __   __   __

26. 66   67   __   __   __

27. 48   49   __   __   __

Write the time.

28. ___:___   ___:___   ___:___

Count the money. Circle the correct amount.

29. 21¢   16¢   30¢

Add or subtract to find the answers.

30. 6 + 6 = __   31. 0 + 3 = __   32. 7 + 1 = __

33. 8 + 1 + 2 = __   34. 4 + 4 + 4 = __   35. 8 - 6 = __

Read the graph.

36. Which drink did the most children have?

○ milk   ○ juice   ○ water

	milk	juice	water
	x		
	x		x
	x	x	x
	x	x	x
	x	x	x
	x	x	x

milk   juice   water

Answer Key

~~~~~~

Beginning-of-Summer Pretest

Page 98
1. fast
2. throw
3. where
4. smile
5. rainbow
6. starfish
7. looking
8. little

Page 99
9. true
10. false
11. true
12. center picture
13. bone, kite, tube, cake

Page 100
14. b, c, d
15. J, K, L
16. n, o, p
17. S, T, U
18. goat
19. sled
20. I went to the book fair.
21. Did you go, too?
22. 12
23. 30
24. 59
25. 36
26. 4 + 0 = 4
27. 7 + 5 = 12
28. 4 + 4 = 8
29. 3 + 2 + 7 = 12
30. 6 - 4 = 2
31. 11 - 3 = 8
32. 6:00
33. 3:30
34. 4:45
35. 17¢

End-of-Summer Posttest

Page 101
1. The Raccoons' Feast
2. a young raccoon
3. at night
4. slide
5. light
6. rain
7. Circle: sleep/keep, pole/mole, air/care, chalk/talk
8. glass
9. hen
10. bug
11. cage
12. feet
13. cube

Page 102
14. wet
15. rough
16. cupcake, notebook, cowboy
17. sleeping
18. happy
19. climb
20. lake
21. d, e, f, g, h, i, j, k, l, m
22. P, Q, R, S, T, U, V, W

Page 103
23. This is my book.
24. Which book do you have?
25. 14, 15, 16, 17, 18
26. 66, 67, 68, 69, 70
27. 48, 49, 50, 51, 52
28. 1:00, 12:15, 7:30
29. 16¢
30. 6 + 6 = 12
31. 0 + 3 = 3
32. 7 + 1 = 8
33. 8 + 1 + 2 = 11
34. 4 + 4+ 4 = 12
35. 8 - 6 = 2
36. milk

hate

under

cry

in

boy

up

dull

open

narrow

happy

low

right

small

good

short

wet

slow

hot

go

smooth

out

laugh

over

love

close

sharp

down

girl

left

high

sad

wide

dry

tall

bad

big

rough

stop

cold

fast

Rhymes with "stall"

fall, call, tell, tale

Rhymes with "shell"

mall, fell, meal, spell

Rhymes with "lake"

stack, steak, make, strap

Rhymes with "door"

store, tour, bow, more

Rhymes with "town"

stow, crown, down, stone

Rhymes with "strip"

drip, trip, stripe, lip

Rhymes with "like"

lick, hike, lake, strike

Rhymes with "jump"

lamp, stump, clump, clamp

Rhymes with "meat"

street, great, greet, leaf

Rhymes with "trout"

pout, thought, clot, stout

fell, spell

Long or short?
c**a**pe   s**a**ve

fall, call

Long or short?
s**a**ck   **a**pple

store, more

Long or short?
p**o**t   st**o**p

steak, make

Long or short?
b**o**at   st**o**ve

drip, trip, lip

Long or short?
sl**ee**p   r**e**al

crown, down

Long or short?
m**e**t   cr**e**pt

stump, clump

Long or short?
umbrella   **u**nder

hike, strike

Long or short?
universe   **u**nicorn

pout, stout

Long or short?
b**i**g   tr**i**p

street, greet

Long or short?
str**i**pe   cl**i**mb

6:30

12:00

5:15

7:00

1:30

4:15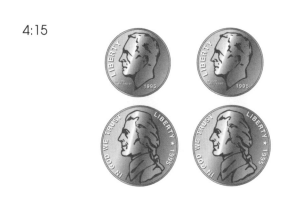

3:00

8:15

11:30

9:00

13¢

23¢

17¢

17¢

30¢

30¢

36¢

28¢

25¢

25¢

15	14
$1 + 4$	$7 + 2$
12	13
$6 + 4$	$2 + 5$
4	12
$3 + 3$	$1 + 5$
12	15
$6 + 0$	$5 + 5$
5	10
$8 + 2$	$9 + 1$

9

$$11 + 3$$

5

$$10 + 5$$

7

$$6 + 7$$

10

$$7 + 5$$

6

$$6 + 6$$

6

$$2 + 2$$

10

$$2 + 13$$

6

$$9 + 3$$

10

$$10 + 0$$

10

$$2 + 3$$

Numbers 1-100

1	2	3	4	5	6	7	8	9	10
11	12	13	14	15	16	17	18	19	20
21	22	23	24	25	26	27	28	29	30
31	32	33	34	35	36	37	38	39	40
41	42	43	44	45	46	47	48	49	50
51	52	53	54	55	56	57	58	59	60
61	62	63	64	65	66	67	68	69	70
71	72	73	74	75	76	77	78	79	80
81	82	83	84	85	86	87	88	89	90
91	92	93	94	95	96	97	98	99	100

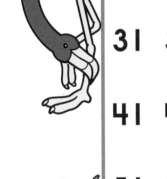
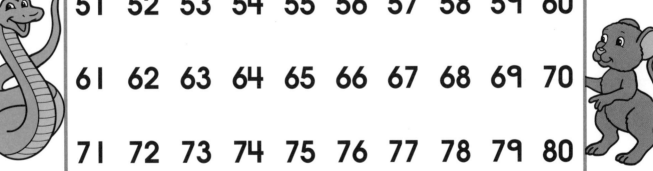

VOWELS

Short

apple
ă

elephant
ĕ

ĭ
insect

octopus
ŏ

ŭ
umbrella

Long

ā
ape

ē
easel

ī
ice cream

oboe
ō

ū
uniform